THEY THINK THAT I DON'T LISTEN

D. STEWART

THEY THINK THAT I DON'T LISTEN

They Think That I Don't Listen gently unveils the layers of Auditory Processing Disorder, making it accessible and relatable to children.

It's not just a story about struggles with sound and communication; it's a tale of perseverance, understanding, and the power of patience and support from family, friends, and teachers.

People think that I don't listen. That I don't try or I don't care. But I really do my best. The words get jumbled up and I miss some things they say. I'm listening, my brain just doesn't always hear.

I have Auditory Processing

Disorder.

That means even though I can

hear, I can't understand

everything the same way

other people do. It can impact

my memory, learning, and

confidence.

To me, it feels like I'm trying to listen to my favorite song on the radio, but the signal keeps getting mixed up with other stations. The static and interference makes it hard to understand the music clearly.

My friends are playing a game
and I just can't understand the
rules. I want to ask again, but I
know they won't want to
explain it another time.
Instead, I pretend I don't want
to play.

I try to keep track of my things, but still it all gets lost. I come to school with lots of stuff and can't find any of it by the end of the day.

I'm worried I'll get in trouble and being nervous makes it even harder to find my things.

It doesn't seem to matter how

many times I read the

directions, I still don't know

where to start. It's too many

words that don't make sense

to me and no clear place to

begin. I'm overwhelmed and

think I'll never get this done.

No matter how much I try to keep up in class, I always fall behind. The teacher is talking fast, kids are making noise, and my notes are messy. I can't go out and play until I sort it all out. I'm sad to see everyone having fun when I am stuck inside.

My coach says I'm an amazing athlete but I just can't run the plays right. I try to understand the directions but I just can't seem to remember which way to go and when. I keep trying but I feel lost when everyone else seems to know what to do.

Things everyone else can do by

the time they are my age, just

seem impossible for me. I can

try it out a hundred times and

all I do is fail. Why can't

anything come easy for me?

My answers don't come

quickly and people think it's

because I wasn't paying

attention. They ask me a

question and want a fast

answer. If it's not quick,

I must be daydreaming.

But that's not it at all.

I read the page ten times and I still can't remember what it was about. The story seems like fun, but it gets confusing as I read. It makes me want to quit and I think there will never be a book for me.

When I feel like giving up, I remember that I am loved by many people and they are on my side. They've found ways that they can support me and I'm not alone.

Sometimes I learn best with pictures and lists. I can build my habits and routines by being able to see and check off what I need. Especially if these are hung up around the house where I can see them.

When I misplace my things,

it's by accident. It makes me

upset too. The best thing to do

is treat me gently and help me

find a solution. We can label

my supplies and belongings

together so they are easier for

someone to return to me.

**IF FOUND
PLEASE RETURN TO:**

If you ask me a question, give me time to answer. I want to help pick the movie out too, but I'm giving it lots of thought. Smile while you wait and I will feel at ease.

I want to be in fun activities and try to learn new things. Performing sounds fun but I need more explanation than what I get in class. Slow it down and show me again when it's quiet and I can practice.

Studying sounds easy but knowing how to do it is hard. Help me make flashcards and show me different techniques. The more creative ways I can study, the better I will remember.

If I can't figure out where to start, I like when my teacher gives me directions in a different way.

Their smile always helps and they never ask why I wasn't listening or look mad as they help me understand.

Playing the audiobook while I read along helps me understand better. It paints the picture more clearly in my mind. If the book is also a movie, I watch it first so I can visualize the characters and the settings.

BEFORE I learn about something new, my teachers can let me know what we will be working on next. Then at home I can watch videos and learn the vocabulary When the lessons starts in class, I have a good foundation.

Explaining what I need or asking a question can be hard. Being able to email my teacher helps. I can take extra time to think about my question and what I need. It shows my teachers I care about my work and their reply shows they care about me.

E-mail!

Working with my friends in a

small group can help me

understand. With patient and

kind kids around, I can ask lots

of questions. Many friends are

eager to share their notes and

what they know.

I want to play new games and

try out different activities. But

the best way for me to be able

to understand the rules is to

show me how it's done.

Let me watch for a minute and

then join in once I'm clear on

what to do.

Even if I fall behind, know that

I am trying. Please don't take

away the fun parts of the day

just so I can catch up. The

breaks and time to burn off my

energy are an important part

of my day.

When I am watching a video or television, it is helpful for me to be able to used closed captioning. I can read along and fill in pieces I may have missed.

Explaining things to me is important and so is how you do it. Make sure you have my attention and I can see your face. Be patient as I try to understand.

And most of all please remind

me as often as you can, that I

am more than just one thing.

More than my grades. More

than the things I forget and

lose. Or the way I fall behind. I

am a whole person. I am more

than a kid that people think

 doesn't listen.

Auditory Processing Disorder is complex and can present in many different ways.

In the pages of this book, Author Danielle Stewart shares the perspective and tips she's learned as a parent of a child with APD. With the feedback of many other caregivers and children with learning differences, she hopes this resource will serve as a place for representation of shared feelings and experience as well as strategies that might help navigating with APD.

Patience, Kindness and Accommodations can make all the difference!

For more resources see the links below:

https://www.asha.org/public/hearing/understanding-auditory-processing-disorders-in-children/

https://www.childrenshospital.org/conditions/auditory-processing-disorder

ALSO BY D. STEWART

24392081R00038